DEBBI FIELDS

The
Cookie
Lady

DEBBI FIELDS

The Cookie Lady

Harriet Spiesman

GEC GARRETT EDUCATIONAL CORPORATION

Cover: *Debbi Fields.* (Rick Mahan.)

Edited and produced by Synthegraphics Corporation

Library of Congress Cataloging in Publication Data

Spiesman, Harriet, 1932-
  Debbi Fields : the cookie lady / Harriet Spiesman.
    p. cm. — (Wizards of business)
  Includes index.
  Summary: A biography of the energetic girl whose enthusiasm, ideas, and hard work helped her become a world famous "cookie lady."
  ISBN 1-56074-015-9
  1. Fields, Debbi—Juvenile literature.   2. Women in business—United States—Biography—Juvenile literature. 3. Cookie industry—United States—Juvenile literature. 4. Fields, Debbi. [1. Women in business.   2. Cookie industry.] I. Title. II. Series.
HD9058.C65F547 1992
338.7'6647525'092—dc20
[B]

91-32783
CIP
AC

Contents

Chronology for **Debbi Fields**

1956	Born on September 18 in Oakland, California
1974	Graduated from Alameda High School
1976	Married Randy Fields on September 21
1977	Opened first cookie store in Palo Alto, California, August 18
1979	Opened second store in San Francisco
1979-1981	Expanded to thirty stores in the United States
1981	Moved family and company to Park City, Utah
1982-1986	Continued expansion in United States, Japan, Hong Kong, Australia, England, and Canada
1987	Company stock offered on London Stock Exchange; co-authored book, *One Smart Cookie;* purchased La Petite Boulangerie bakery chain
1989	Operated 486 stores; $118.4 million in sales
1990	Member of Board of Governors of LDS Hospital and Primary Children's Foundation Medical Center, Salt Lake City, Utah; founder and director of Mrs. Fields Children's Health Foundation

Chapter 1

Starting from Scratch

Ball girl for the Oakland A's. Bouncy Christmas elf at Mervyn's Department Store. A dolphin's teammate at Marine World. Beginning with her first job for the Oakland A's, Debbi Sivyer had boundless energy for the workplace. Strange as it may seem, these were the jobs that helped her become the world-famous "cookie lady" known as Mrs. Fields!

When she was thirteen, Debbi wanted new snow skis. Her parents couldn't afford such luxuries, but that was no problem. She had been raised to believe that if she was willing to work hard, she could earn whatever she wanted.

Debbi watched as her four older sisters worked for the special things they wanted. This seemed fair. It didn't bother her that some of the kids at school came from wealthier families. As long as there was a way for her to earn money for the skis, she was eager to go to work.

Her sister Mary helped Debbi get her first job. Mary worked in the office of the Oakland Athletics baseball team. The A's had decided to hire girls instead of boys to retrieve balls hit along the foul line, and Mary suggested that Debbi apply for the job. At thirteen, Debbi was a high-spirited tomboy. She just knew she would be perfect for the job. Her enthusiasm must have convinced the A's. She was hired to catch foul balls between third base and the stands.

THE SWEET TASTE OF SUCCESS

Never mind that she didn't know how to catch a baseball, Debbi was delighted with her special baseball outfit and mitt! She lunged after each foul hit her way, beaming when she finally managed to toss it back to the umpire. This spunky bundle of energy put on quite a show, and Debbi was soon well known to the players and the fans.

Whenever a foul ball came her way, Debbi knew all eyes were on her. She discovered that making people laugh and enjoy themselves made her feel wonderful.

Debbi also learned how important it is to treat people with kindness. Some of the stars on the team were very friendly to autograph seekers. Others were not. It especially hurt her to see children treated rudely by their sports heroes. This was a lesson she never forgot: everyone matters and deserves to be treated like a special person.

Debbi's experience with the Oakland A's was her first taste of success. She realized she had a natural ability to make people happy. The public appreciated her enthusiasm and her willingness to take risks. New skis weren't the only reward for her hard work.

FAMILY MATTERS

Debra Jane Sivyer was born on September 18, 1956, to Edward and Mary Casovia Sivyer. Debbi was the youngest of five girls. She grew up in a working-class neighborhood in East Oakland, California. Her parents were Catholic and believed in close families. They lived in a pink stucco house that had once belonged to Debbi's grandparents.

Sivyer was a French name, but there was also a little Czechoslovakian and Cherokee Indian in the family's background. Her mother's parents were from Yugoslavia, where her grandfather had been a successful chef. They settled in California and opened a restaurant in San Francisco, but it was destroyed in the earthquake of 1906.

Debbi's dad, Edward Sivyer, worked as a welder repairing machine parts for the Navy. He loved his job. Money was not a major issue in the Sivyer home. The girls grew up knowing that material possessions don't guarantee happiness.

The small house on East 27th Street had a concrete yard and one bathroom. Imagine five energetic girls sharing one bathroom! It was many years before Debbi had her own room.

But it never occurred to Debbi to think of herself as poor. When she was in high school, she began to meet girls who lived in beautiful homes with swimming pools and fancy furniture. She was fascinated by the luxuries she saw, but she couldn't understand how the girls could take it all for granted. She discovered that their wealth didn't make them any happier. For years she had been hearing her dad say, "My wealth has never been in money – it's been found in my family and friends." She realized he was right!

Everyone pitched in to help with the housework. Ironing, cleaning, and packing lunches were part of the everyday routine. Doing things together was fun and an important part of growing up.

A Special Child

Debbi's biggest problem as the youngest daughter was keeping up with her sisters. Linda, Mary, Marlene, and Cathy were lively, **competitive** girls. (Terms in **boldface type** are defined in the Glossary at the back of the book.) They seemed to get all the attention.

It wasn't easy being the fifth girl in the family, especially when Debbi knew her father had been hoping for a boy. Debbi was determined to be as special to him as the son he would never have. Her solution was to become a gutsy little tomboy.

When she was quite small, Debbi's dad built her a souped-up bicycle out of spare parts. Off she'd go, barreling down the street, scaring her poor mother out of her wits. There was no way Debbi was going to sit around waiting for something to happen. She made her own excitement, rushing head-first through life. One way or another, Debbi Sivyer was going to be noticed.

Unfortunately, what her sisters saw was a pesky baby sister doing dumb things to get their attention. Before long they were calling her "the dumb one," and for years that's how Debbi thought of herself.

SCHOOL DAYS

School was a real challenge for Debbi. Like her sisters, Debbi attended strict Catholic schools. Sitting still in class was boring, and she amused herself by daydreaming or figuring out ways to test the rules.

If the dress code called for skirts to be a certain length, she made sure hers were just a little shorter. She discovered that if she could make the nuns laugh, they were less likely to punish her.

As Debbi says in her own book, *One Smart Cookie,* this idea intrigued her: "If I can entertain people, make them happy, I'll be a success."

In the Sivyer home, A's and B's didn't matter as much as learning how to be a good person.

Seeking Acceptance

Debbi was just an average student, and she didn't do much better on the social scene. She wanted to fit in with the girls at school, but the harder she tried to get their attention, the less they liked her. Today she admits she was "the world's worst follower."

While the rest of the kids were dressing alike, acting alike, and following the crowd, Debbi was trying to stand out by being different. She couldn't figure out what she was doing wrong. She was pretty, but her good looks did little to overcome the pain of feeling stupid and rejected.

In spite of these challenges, Debbi was an outgoing, enthusiastic child. She was surrounded by a fun-loving, caring family.

PLEASING THE PUBLIC

Debbi's job with the Oakland A's had given her confidence. Hard work brought her the recognition she craved, and pleasing people made her feel great.

When she was fifteen, Debbi took a part-time job at Mervyn's Department Store. She was supposed to be a salesperson in the boys' section, but she threw herself into reorganizing the department. The stock, the sales tables, the service had to be perfect. She wanted her customers to enjoy shopping, and that meant giving each one special attention.

In the Limelight

Recognizing a good thing when they saw it, the store managers made Debbi an elf during the Christmas season. Prancing through the store in tights, little elf boots, and a tasseled hat, she charmed reluctant children into having their pictures taken with Santa.

When she was seventeen, Debbi got a job water-skiing and performing with the dolphins at Marine World. Never one to turn down a challenge, she joined the human pyramid that zipped through the water on skis for the grand finale.

COOKIE CHAMP

The kitchen was the Sivyer sisters' favorite gathering place. Mrs. Sivyer did all the cooking, but the girls enjoyed baking. Mary baked the family cakes, Cathy served up pancakes; and, at thirteen, Debbi discovered her talent for baking cookies. She was fond of chocolate and concentrated her efforts on chocolate chip cookies. At last, Debbi had found something she did better than her sisters.

A Delicious Mistake

Chocolate chip cookies, or Toll House cookies as they were originally called, were invented in 1930 by Ruth Wakefield. Mrs. Wakefield owned a popular restaurant in Whitman, Massachusetts, called the Toll House Inn.

One day, as she was preparing to bake her Butter Drop Do cookies, Mrs. Wakefield decided to add a chopped-up chocolate bar. She expected the pieces to melt and turn the cookies chocolaty and brown. Instead, the chocolate bits just became soft. Her "mistake" was an instant hit with the restaurant guests. Before long, everyone was baking chocolate chip cookies.

Debbi was too creative to leave the recipe alone. The first change she made was to switch from margarine to butter. With so many mouths to feed, Mrs. Sivyer usually bought margarine because it cost less than butter.

As a teenager, Debbi discovered that the secret to baking great cookies was to use the very best ingredients. By then, she was working part time, so she used her own money to buy butter. She wanted her cookies to be perfect. The family couldn't gulp them down fast enough. Batch after batch disappeared straight from the oven. Debbi was a hit with her soft, chewy cookies!

Chapter 2

Mrs. Who?

When Debbi was seventeen, she graduated from Alameda High School. She hadn't put much effort into studying, and her grades showed it. Her only notable success in high school was being chosen Homecoming Queen. But she hadn't really been popular. Debbi didn't date much, and she had never belonged to any particular groups of friends. She didn't know what she would do next, but she was relieved to be through with school.

Debbi describes this time as her "dark period." She had no serious goals. All she really wanted was to be on her own and earn enough money so that she could go skiing. She spent the next two years living at home and working in retail stores. Whenever she saved enough money, she took off for the ski slopes.

RANDY FIELDS

It was during this time that Debbi met Randy Fields. She was returning from a ski trip, and they were both stranded at the airport in Denver, Colorado. Randy spotted Debbi in a phone booth and introduced himself. He was determined to know this beautiful, vivacious young woman.

Debbi's first impression of Randy was that he was a rather strange fellow. He had a thick head of unruly hair, and wore square glasses and a huge tie. But he convinced her that he was perfectly respectable, and they talked until their planes were ready to take off.

When she returned to Oakland, Debbi heard from Randy several times a day. He was persistent, and soon they were dating steadily.

A Mismatch?

Randy Fields was ten years older than Debbi. He had been a gifted child, successfully investing in stocks and bonds when he was only eleven years old. He graduated from Stanford University with top honors, and started his own investment company when he was twenty-one.

Randy had earned a reputation as a brilliant **financial consultant.** People all over the world sought his advice, and *Time* and *Newsweek* magazines published articles about him.

They couldn't have been a more unlikely couple. Debbi was eighteen, Randy was twenty-eight. They were from different religious backgrounds. She had squeaked through high school, he had piled up degrees and honors at Stanford.

FOR BETTER OR WORSE

Randy and Debbi fell head over heels in love. For the first time in her life, someone took Debbi seriously, listened to her ideas, and made her feel important. On September 21, 1976, they were married.

At first, Debbi was caught up in the novelty of being a housewife. But soon she grew restless. She had never lost her strong desire to do something worthwhile, to help people in some way. Debbi was an active, energetic person. She needed to do more with her life than just shop, cook, and clean their small apartment.

Back to School

Debbi decided it was time to renew her education. She enrolled at Los Altos Junior College, where she became a serious student and began earning A's. This was a brand new experience for her!

While Debbi was attending Los Altos, Randy's job required that the two of them get together frequently with his business associates. They were high-powered, important people, and they expected Randy Field's wife to be a bright, accomplished woman.

Debbi had nothing in common with Randy's associates; nothing to talk about. Santa's merry little elf was not going to impress this crowd! Sure enough, as soon as they discovered she was merely a housewife and part-time student, they wrote her off as a nobody. Debbi felt like a big zero.

The Big Put-Down

Debbi's worst moment came on a trip to New York. She and Randy were invited to the home of a person who was famous for putting together huge business deals.

The visit had barely begun when their host started asking Debbi questions about herself. What was she doing? What were her plans? She was nervous, tried to be clever, and he grew impatient. Finally, he snapped, "What *do* you intend to do with your life?"

Poor Debbi! Trying to sound sophisticated, she mispronounced a word. Her rude host tossed a dictionary in her lap and suggested she learn how to use the English language. Totally humiliated, Debbi struggled to control her tears. She couldn't spoil this visit for Randy.

A TURNING POINT

Randy's friends had acted as if Debbi wasn't good enough for them, and she had assumed they were right. How could she expect others to respect her if she didn't respect herself? The truth was, she *didn't* know what she wanted to do with her life!

Debbi was determined to prove that she could be more than Randy Fields' tag-along wife. She needed to make her own contribution. But what?

Debbi's father had taught her that to be successful, you must do something because you love it, not just for the money. He had always advised, "Be the best you can be."

Debbi certainly loved baking cookies, and she knew she was good at it. After years of experimenting, she believed she made the best cookie she had ever tasted. Her recipe contained the finest butter, pure vanilla, nuts, and, most important, almost as many cups of rich chocolate as flour. The result was a soft, chewy, chocolate chip delight.

Debbi's cookies were Randy's favorite dessert, so she baked several batches a week. With fresh-baked cookies in the house all the time, Debbi couldn't resist nibbling away at them. In fact, she admits she developed her talent to bake cookies from years of sampling so many.

Randy teased Debbi about how many cookies she ate each day. So she started to make them bigger. Now she could say she ate only two instead of six! The larger cookies were even more delicious.

Randy began taking Debbi's cookies to the office. His clients loved them. Soon they were expecting cookie breaks before getting down to business.

For some time, Debbi had toyed with the idea of opening her own cookie shop. As she watched her family and friends gobbling up her cookies, she became convinced she could sell them.

TAKING A CHANCE

In 1977, the idea of a cookie store was just plain crazy. At least, that's what all the **marketing** experts said. There were more than enough bakeries and supermarkets already selling cookies. A store that just sold cookies was doomed to fail.

Furthermore, all the marketing surveys showed that Americans preferred small, crisp, crunchy cookies. Debbi's were large, soft, and chewy. No matter who she asked, everyone told Debbi the same thing, "Don't do it, it will never work!"

But Debbi was stubbornly convinced she had a good idea. And she had her own theories about shoppers. She believed that people wanted shopping to be fun, not just a mad dash up and down the aisles, grabbing merchandise off the shelves.

Debbi also remembered how the public had responded to her enthusiasm when she worked for the A's and at Mervyn's Department Store and Marine World. Most people might not go out of their way to find excitement or something new and different, but they sure enjoyed it when it was offered to them.

Perhaps it was just a crazy dream: Debbi Fields in her own small, friendly shop, serving up freshly baked cookies, and making sure each customer left with a special "feel-good feeling." But there were plenty of people out there whose crazy ideas had turned out to be hugely successful.

Although Randy's business sense told him Debbi was headed for failure, he realized how important it was for her to have this opportunity to prove herself. Together, they ignored all the experts' advice and decided to go into business.

Finding a Location

Randy figured they would need about $50,000 to get started. Many bankers were just as negative as everyone else and turned down their request for a loan. Who was Mrs. Fields? She had no business education, no business experience, and she had

Debbi Fields' dream was to sell freshly baked cookies in her own cookie store. (Rich Mahan.)

a nutty idea about selling something anyone could make in their own kitchen.

The loan officers at Bank of America weren't any more optimistic, but they admired Debbi's confidence and determination. They also loved her cookies! They were willing to give her a chance. They trusted her to pay back the loan.

After the loan papers were signed, Debbi read every book in the library on how to start a small business. She spent two months learning how to be an **entrepreneur.**

The first thing the store needed was a name. She liked The Chocolate Chippery, but it didn't seem personal enough. Randy suggested Mrs. Fields Chocolate Chippery. That sounded just right.

Debbi's next job was finding a place to rent. Shopping centers were springing up across the country. She recognized the advantage of being in an enclosed center or mall. Convenient parking facilities and year-round, one-stop shopping attract many people to shopping centers. They could be Debbi's potential customers.

Around the turn of the century, department store retailers introduced tearooms in their stores for the convenience of their customers. Since then, snack foods have become part of the shopping experience. Debbi reasoned that busy shoppers or people just strolling through a shopping center would welcome a cookie break. So she looked for space in a mall.

Setting Up Shop

She found an empty store in Liddicoat's Market, a shopping **arcade** in Palo Alto, California. Liddicoat's was an international food arcade. Debbi rented space in the back, between a delicatessen and a shop she describes as "sort of Tibetan."

Growth of Shopping Malls

> After World War II, millions of Americans moved from big cities to the suburbs. As the suburbs grew, shopping habits changed. Downtown business centers were no longer convenient for families who lived many miles from the city. Many stores moved out to the suburbs. Real estate developers built suburban shopping centers and malls to accommodate the new trend in **retailing.**

She couldn't afford new equipment, so Debbi went bargain hunting for used ovens, sinks, and other baking equipment. Many kind friends and workmen helped her prepare the new store. Debbi says she could never have opened without their generous support.

There were, however, some suppliers who were not as cooperative. When she tried to order a small amount of chocolate from a large company, the salesman let her know he wasn't interested in anything less than a 10,000-pound order.

The next salesman Debbi called had exactly the opposite attitude. His company was also a large and famous chocolate manufacturer. But he came right out to the store with a variety of chocolate samples, gave Debbi some helpful advice, and treated her like a valuable customer. He sold Debbi only twenty-five pounds of chocolate that day. But she appreciated his kindness and remained a loyal customer. Today, Mrs. Fields still buys chocolate from him – millions of dollars worth each year.

By August 1977, Debbi had tested and tasted hundreds of cookies. As she recalls in her book, when she first told her parents she wanted to open a cookie store, her mother said, "Debbi, I can't believe you're going to waste your life standing over a hot stove."

Well, here she was, about to do just that. Mrs. Fields Chocolate Chippery was ready to open for business.

Chapter 3

Mrs. Fields, That's Who!

In 1977, President Jimmy Carter was warning Americans about the energy crisis. Elvis Presley, "King of Rock 'n Roll" died. Voyager I and Voyager II began exploring outer space. Leonid Brezhnev was elected President of the Soviet Union. That same year, Debbi Fields was twenty years old, and on August 18 she began her career as Mrs. Fields, "the cookie lady."

CRUMBLING SPIRITS

On August 17, the night before her first day of business, Debbi was in a panic. For weeks she had been telling herself the experts were wrong. Even if they weren't, the worst thing that could happen was that she would have to close the store. It wouldn't be a personal failure. It would be a business failure. She could always get a job to pay back the loan.

Now, only hours before the store was to open, Debbi was overcome with doubts. Who was she, Debbi Fields, to think she could do what everyone said was impossible? She spent the night in tears, with Randy trying to cheer her up. Jokingly, he bet her that she wouldn't take in fifty dollars by the end of the first day. He knew Debbi was so competitive she'd do everything possible to win the bet.

At six o'clock in the morning of August 18, Debbi arrived at the store. She was scared and exhausted from lack of sleep; but the cookies had to be baked for the nine o'clock opening.

Debbi had decided to offer seven varieties of cookies: milk chocolate with and without nuts, semisweet chocolate with and without nuts, oatmeal raisin nut, chocolate brownies, and carob cookies. Carob was a sweet substitute for people who didn't eat chocolate.

The store wasn't air-conditioned. Debbi had dressed in a crisp white shirt, brown slacks, and a bright yellow apron. For a cheerful effect, she had added a perky straw hat. Between the heat outside and the ovens going full blast inside, the shop soon became hot and sticky.

Not a Nibble

The cookies were carefully arranged on the counter. Everything was in order. There was nothing left for Debbi to do but wait for her first customer. Forcing a brave smile on her face, she waited. And waited, and waited.

By noon, Mrs. Fields Chocolate Chippery hadn't sold a single cookie. A few shoppers in the arcade wandered in, but when they heard the price, twenty-five cents each, they lost interest and left.

A whole morning of failure was just about all Debbi could stand. Feeling desperate, she called her friend Ann to help bail her out. Ann rushed over and they worked out a plan.

The whole point of the shop was to serve soft cookies fresh from the oven. If the cookies sat out for more than several hours, they would become too hard. They weren't meant to last for days, like store-bought cookies.

Giving Away Samples

Staring glumly at the full trays, Debbi knew she had to act fast. If the customers didn't think her cookies were worth twenty-five cents, she would change their minds. She would give away samples!

Leaving Ann to watch the store, Debbi grabbed a tray of cookies and started walking through the shopping arcade. But she couldn't even talk people into taking freebies!

By this time, Debbi was terrified of failure. She knew she would never forgive herself if she gave up. Debbi went out into the street and began walking up and down, begging strangers to try her cookies. Her courage paid off. Pretty soon she had emptied several trays. And sure enough, satisfied people followed her back to the store to buy more.

By the end of the day, Debbi had won her bet. Mrs. Fields first store had sold exactly seventy-five dollars worth of cookies!

THE COMPETITIVE EDGE

When Debbi went into the street with cookie samples, she had no idea she had stumbled onto a valuable marketing strategy. Like any retailer in a **free market economy,** Debbi had to persuade the public to buy cookies from her instead of from the **competition.**

Debbi Fields' competitors were the bakeries and stores in Palo Alto that were already selling cookies. But her cookies were distinctly different. What she needed to do was **promote** them.

Sampling gave people an opportunity to compare Mrs. Fields' cookies with the cookies they usually ate. It gave Debbi a chance to communicate with **consumers** in a direct and

Competition

Retailers not only compete to sell products, they also compete for customers. Competition benefits retailers and consumers. It helps keep prices down. Competition also helps regulate quality and service.

Retailers compete by promoting their products. Advertising and special sales are forms of promotion. To compete successfully, retailers must also maintain quality. If customers are not satisfied with the quality of a product, they will switch to a competitor's product.

friendly way. And it increased sales. Sampling was so successful that it eventually became a regular custom in all of Mrs. Fields' stores.

A Nice Place to Visit

Another competitive advantage Debbi had was the type of store she created. As a young housewife, she had discovered that there were very few small, family-owned stores. Most shopping was done in huge self-service supermarkets.

Debbi preferred shopping in smaller stores. She appreciated the friendly atmosphere and special service she received. The store owners and clerks were always eager to be helpful.

Debbi believed shoppers would welcome a change from the impersonal supermarkets. She made a determined effort to give her **specialty store** a warm, inviting feeling. Debbi worked hard to make everyone feel special.

Many people soon became regular customers, stopping in every morning at Debbi's store for coffee and cookies. Every day, more and more people came in to buy her cookies. Pretty soon, Debbi needed help.

ESTABLISHING AN IMAGE

The store became so busy that Debbi had to hire an assistant. As she added to her staff, Debbi developed her own management style. Most of the policies she started in her first store are still practiced today at all of her stores.

Debbi's enthusiasm, friendliness, and concern for each customer has helped her create the Mrs. Fields **image.** She wasn't just in the cookie business; she was in the people business. Debbi made sure her employees shared her personal qualities and her attitude about work.

Debbi knew her employees could have a tremendous effect on the store's image. Courteous, friendly service would encourage customers to return often.

Since she was spending twelve hours a day in the store, Debbi thought of her co-workers as a second family. They must care about each other, have a good time, and, above all, love their work. Debbi encouraged them to become completely involved in the business.

In the Palo Alto store, the staff set up hourly sales goals and competed to see who could sell the most cookies. To keep from getting bored, they took turns at each job. Everyone mixed dough, dropped dough onto the baking sheets, watched the ovens, sold cookies, and cleaned up – including Debbi.

The Best Cookie

The most important rule at Mrs. Fields was "bake the best cookie!" Every now and then, someone would try to convince Debbi to save money by using less expensive ingredients. She always refused. If she could taste the difference, so could her customers. Debbi's goal was not to sell the most cookies; her goal was to sell the *best* cookies.

A good example of Debbi's commitment to quality oc-

The Mrs. Fields image is delicious cookies and a feel-good feeling.
(Busath Photography.)

curred about six months after she opened the Palo Alto store. Too much rain had destroyed the California raisin crop. Debbi needed raisins for her raisin oatmeal nut cookies. Debra Specials, as they were called, were one of her most popular cookies.

The man who supplied the raisins told Debbi the price would be "sky-high."

"Buy them anyway," she said.

The supplier tried to talk Debbi out of making a costly mistake. He recommended using dates, which were inexpensive.

Debbi was doubtful, she hated dates. But she went out to taste her competitors' raisin cookies. They *were* using dates, and their cookies were terrible! That did it; Debbi ordered the raisins.

Debbi had to raise the price of the Debra Specials to meet her higher cost. But when the customers kept buying them, Debbi was more convinced than ever that people were willing to pay for quality.

The store's policy was to guarantee everything it sold. If a customer wasn't satisfied, the order would be replaced. Debbi's cookies had to be soft and moist. If they weren't sold two hours after baking, they became "cookie orphans." This meant they were donated to the Red Cross and other charities.

Debbi could have saved money by baking a daily supply of cookies all at once. If they were all baked first thing each morning, she would have needed less help. But, earning more **profit** was not her goal. Pleasing the customers was more important.

Spreading Out

Before long, some of Debbi's employees were asking her to consider opening a second store. They were ambitious and wanted more responsibility. A second store would give them a chance to become Mrs. Fields managers.

Shortly after Debbi opened in Palo Alto, she was given an opportunity to expand. One of her customers was the developer of a shopping mall in San Francisco. He loved Debbi's cookies and was certain Mrs. Fields would do well in his mall. But Debbi turned him down. She was content with her little store; and she had her hands full running it.

When the developer contacted her again in 1978, Debbi was ready to say yes. Although she and Randy had some concerns about expanding, they agreed they should accept the offer. They didn't think it would be good for the business to stand still. Also, expansion would give Debbi's loyal co-workers an opportunity they had earned.

Debbi had learned how to accept a challenge. Mrs. Fields Cookies was the result of her willingness to take risks. Now she had a chance to turn her small business into a growing company.

Chapter 4

_____

"Good Enough
Never Is"

The rapid growth of Mrs. Fields Cookies was exciting, but it also brought problems. The first few years were stressful. Debbi was giving Mrs. Fields all her time and attention. She and Randy had to adjust their marriage to the demands of a fast-growing business.

Randy was still running his own consulting business, but he was a major contributor to Debbi's success. He taught her the details of bookkeeping, inventory, and taxes. He also began computerizing the business in order to make it run more efficiently.

When Mrs. Fields Cookies became successful, Debbi and

Randy could have chosen to **franchise** the business. Many food and restaurant chains are franchised.

This might have been one way to make her business grow if Debbi's biggest concern was making money. But franchising never appealed to her. Debbi wanted to be sure the products carrying her name were the best, baked by people who took pride in their work. This meant she had to maintain control of all her stores.

MANAGEMENT BY MOTIVATION

The success of Mrs. Fields Cookies is due to Debbi's commitment to quality and her ability to motivate employees. The success of each store depends on the people working in that store. Debbi lets them know how important they are. She hires people who want to grow with the company. Anyone starting out behind the counter has a chance to move up to a vice-presidency.

Every Mrs. Fields executive must spend some time working in one of the stores. Debbi wants everyone to experience mixing, baking, and selling Mrs. Fields cookies. Store managers attend the Cookie College in Park City, Utah, where the company headquarters are now located. The classes are run like pep rallies; Debbi's huge smile and enthusiasm are contagious!

Employees learn how to bake and recognize perfect cookies. They must check each cookie to be sure it's soft, with plenty of chocolate chips sticking up on top. Debbi tells her

Franchising

One form of business ownership is called a franchise. It is the right to sell certain goods or services in a specific area.

Franchising is one way a successful company can expand. The company sells a franchise to someone who will own and operate a branch of the parent company. The parent company (franchiser) provides training, financial assistance, advertising, and other services.

Under the agreement, the buyer (franchisee) has the advantage of starting a new business with a well-known name and reputation. In return, the franchiser usually receives a share of the profits.

people it's OK to make mistakes. Just don't try to sell them to the customers!

Employees are encouraged to take home a certain number of cookies every day. They baked them, so they should share them with their friends and families. This helps build pride in their work.

Checking Up

Debbi Fields travels several days a week. She visits each store at least once a year. Sometimes she pretends she's a casual shopper so she can observe the enthusiasm and service of the

Debbi visits each store at least once a year to be sure the cookies are baked just right. (Rich Mahan.)

staff. She also checks the products. Debbi has been known to throw out hundreds of cookies if they don't meet her high standards.

One day, Debbi walked into a store and spotted a batch of overbaked cookies. She asked the salesman what he thought of them. He said he thought they were good enough. Debbi responded, "Good enough never is." That immediately became the company motto.

Debbi created fourteen cookie recipes for Mrs. Fields. However, the stores offer only seven varieties on any one day. It's up to the employees in each store to decide which varieties their customers prefer.

Secret Recipes

All the Mrs. Fields cookie recipes are top-secret. Debbi created every one at home or in the company's test kitchens. She worked with her suppliers to develop special blends of vanilla, chocolate, sugar, and flour.

The ingredients are prepackaged and shipped under the Mrs. Fields label. Not even store managers know where the ingredients are purchased. The Mrs. Fields organization is a valuable customer. It purchases many tons of baking supplies every year, and suppliers will not reveal the formulas to anyone.

Several years ago, a rumor was started that the company was going to sell its recipe for chocolate chip cookies. This was untrue; Debbi would never sell her recipes to anyone. And even if a recipe did become known, Debbi's cookies couldn't be copied because the ingredients that make them special are available only to her.

Company Goals

Mrs. Fields salespeople are expected to sell a certain number of cookies each hour. Most companies ask their salespeople to meet monthly or yearly **quotas.** But Debbi's own selling experience has taught her that hourly quotas are easier goals to meet. If a salesperson falls short of an hourly quota by a few dollars, he or she can always make up the difference during the day.

Debbi wants her employees to have fun at work. They can go into the street with samples or sing a silly song if they want to. The main thing is to make people happy with Mrs. Fields cookies!

And to encourage them, Debbi sets the example by joining right in. Reporters who interview Debbi say her favorite words are "fun," "exciting," "giving," and "happy."

Learning Local Customs

Sometimes no amount of training can prepare people for special problems. In 1980, Mrs. Fields opened a store on the island of Oahu in Hawaii. For two weeks after the grand opening, business was terrible. No one could figure out what was wrong.

One day, a man who had grown up in Hawaii asked if a kahuna, an Hawaiian priest, had blessed the store. Debbi had never heard of this custom but immediately arranged to have a ceremony.

The kahuna arrived in his ancient headdress, sprinkled water at the entrance, waved a palm leaf, and chanted a prayer. It worked! The customers started coming, and that store became one of the most successful in the Mrs. Fields chain.

When Mrs. Fields Cookies opened in Hong Kong, the salespeople couldn't persuade anyone to try their samples.

Debbi flew to Hong Kong to see if she could solve the problem. She walked the streets with trays of cookies, but no luck.

Later, Debbi went window-shopping and noticed that all the merchandise was laid out very neatly. Her sample cookies had been piled on trays. Debbi bought larger trays and arranged each cookie on a separate piece of paper. The customers in Hong Kong loved the samples as long as they weren't touching each other!

Tastes differ, too. New Yorkers prefer semisweet chocolate; people in Utah want milk chocolate. In general, most people prefer walnuts, but Hawaiians favor macadamia nuts. The Japanese appreciate quality and seem to go for whatever is the top of the line or most expensive product.

COOKIES AND KIDS

As Mrs. Fields Cookies grew, so did Debbi's family. She and Randy had planned to have four or five children. By 1990, they had four daughters: Jessica, Jenessa, Jennifer, and Ashley.

Debbi is a tireless worker and a devoted mother. She refuses to separate her career and family life, so the children often join her on business trips. They help with taste-testing and love to create new recipes.

Debbi Fields is the founder and chief executive officer of a multi-million dollar corporation. But her private office is set up with toys, books, and a crib. It has been like a second home for her girls.

If she has evening meetings, Debbi brings the people home – right into her kitchen. They play with the children, and sometimes even help with the cooking. A visit with the Fields is very casual and relaxed.

Spreading Out in Utah

In 1981, the Fields family and company moved to Park City, a small ski resort in Utah. Randy and Debbi wanted a country-style life with plenty of room for the children, sports, and animals. Randy believes computers and modern communication technology make it possible for them to live in a small town. Businesses no longer have to be located in major cities.

Debbi and Randy have simple tastes. When they aren't working, they relax at home with their daughters. They all enjoy cross-country skiing, hiking, and horseback riding.

Going Public

By 1980, there were three Mrs. Fields stores. By 1981, there were fourteen. And by 1987, only ten years after opening the first shop, Debbi owned over 500 stores in five countries.

The decision to open in foreign markets was a major step for Mrs. Fields. Today, the company sells its products in Japan, Australia, Hong Kong, England, and Canada.

Becoming an international company is very costly, so Debbi and Randy decided to sell shares of **stock** in their company. This would give them the money they needed to expand.

Selling Stock

A company can divide its ownership among many people by issuing shares of stock. The stock may be privately owned—usually by the people who founded and run the company—or it can be sold to the general public.

In order to sell its stock to the public, a company must join a stock exchange. Selling stock is a way for the company to receive **capital** to expand and become more profitable.

Individuals who buy stock are investing in the company. If the company does well, the price of the stock rises; if the company does poorly, the price drops.

In 1987, Mrs. Fields, Inc. was listed on the London Stock Exchange. That year, profits were up, and the price of the stock soared. In 1987, Debbi also wrote a book, *One Smart Cookie*.

MAJOR CHANGES

But the period of tremendous financial growth was coming to an end. When Debbi had to close over ninety stores because they were not successful, she realized that it was time to de-

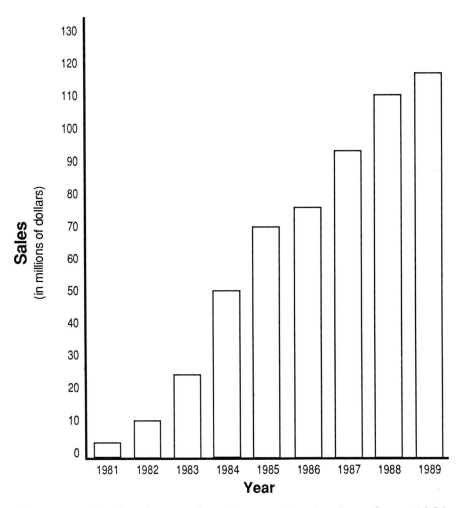

The annual sales figures for Mrs. Fields Cookies from 1981 through 1989.

velop a management team. She hired professional managers to handle the day-to-day operation of the company.

Debbi now concentrates on long-range goals for Mrs. Fields. This means finding new ways to compete in the cookie industry. Debbi and Randy think the answer is in adding brands and products.

Mrs. Fields began **diversifying** in 1987 by purchasing La Petite Boulangerie, a national bakery chain. Debbi also developed muffin and candy recipes and added them to her line.

In 1990, Debbi signed an agreement with a division of the Marriott Corporation. Marriott planned to open at least sixty Mrs. Fields stores in airports and highway plazas. Ambrosia Chocolate has agreed to make and sell Mrs. Fields Chocolate Chips. Debbi is also hoping to open in-store bakeries in some supermarkets.

A Chain of Bakeries

Debbi's most ambitious plan is to develop Mrs. Fields Bakeries. The bakeries will offer muffins, cookies, bread, soups, and sandwiches. There are now fifteen Mrs. Fields Bakery Cookie Cafes, and all are doing well. Debbi hopes to open 250 more by 1995.

David Liederman, creator of David's Cookies, is one of Mrs. Fields' major competitors. He says Debbi is on the right track, that diversification is the way to go.

The future looks bright. Total sales for all the Mrs. Fields divisions were $121 million in 1989. Once Debbi dreamed of owning the best specialty cookie store; now she wants to develop the best specialty bakeries. She seems well on the way to achieving her goal.

Chapter 5

Computers and Cookies

Randy Fields is called "Mrs. Fields' Secret Ingredient." Soon after Debbi opened her second store, Randy began computerizing the company.

Randy is as excited about computers as Debbi is about cookies. For Mrs. Fields Cookies, he created a computer system that is entirely new to the business world. When Randy installed his system, he had two main goals.

First, he wanted to reduce the amount of time employees spend on paperwork and telephone calls. Randy believes machines should do as much work as possible. People should be left free to spend their time creatively.

Randy's second goal was to provide prompt, frequent

communication between each store and the Park City head-quarters. Mrs. Fields, Inc. has hundreds of cookie stores and bakeries. They are spread across the United States and five other countries.

VISITING BY COMPUTER

Debbi cannot possibly visit all the stores more than once or twice a year. But she wants them to run as if she was right there supervising the work crews. Randy's computer system allows Debbi to maintain control over her stores.

Each Mrs. Fields store has an inexpensive personal computer. These machines are linked up with the big computers at Park City headquarters. This puts Debbi and her staff in daily contact with each store.

The Day Planner

Randy has designed a software program called the Day Planner. This program gives each store manager a daily plan. Here's how it works.

When the manager arrives at the store in the morning, he spends about twenty minutes at the computer keyboard. He punches up the Day Planner to help him organize his hourly tasks. The program asks him several questions: What day of the week is it? Is it a holiday? Is it a school day? Is it a normal day? What's the weather?

A complete **data base** of facts about the shop's history is already stored in the computer. It will tell the manager how much business to expect on this particular type of day.

For instance, if it's a rainy Wednesday and a school day, the computer will plan each hour of the day. It uses the information it has about other rainy Wednesdays. It will tell the manager how much dough to mix, when to mix it, how many customers to expect, and how many cookies the store must sell to meet its hourly quota.

Store managers could make these estimates on paper, but the computer saves hours of time. Also, since so much information is stored in the computer's memory, its estimates are probably more accurate.

Every hour, the manager enters current sales figures. Depending on how the store is doing, the computer might change plans for the next hour. For example, if sales are too low, it might suggest giving away samples. If necessary, the program might tell the crew to bake fewer cookies. This helps cut down on waste and saves money.

The computer also helps in other ways. It figures out how many store employees the manager will need for each two-week period. This means the manager won't be caught with too few workers. And he avoids paying for help he doesn't really need.

More Computer Power

Randy even created an interview program that managers can use when they hire new workers. Each person applying for a job answers a series of questions. The program checks the answers and suggests which person will be best for each job. Of course, the manager always makes the final decision.

Another program helps solve equipment problems. If a mixer in a New York store isn't working properly, the store manager calls up the repair program in the computer. It tells the manager what to check and how he or she might solve the problem.

If the mixer still doesn't work, the store computer then sends a repair request to the main computer in Park City. The big computer receives all the necessary information: which machine is broken, past problems with the mixer, and which repair service to call.

The Park City computer makes all the arrangements for the repairs to be done in New York. When the mixer is fixed, the New York manager enters a message that it's OK to pay the bill.

Automatic Ordering

Randy Fields says the goal in retailing is to keep people close to people. Employees should not spend time on any job a machine can do as well. People should do only what the computer is unable to do.

Because the computer knows a store's baking history for each year, it can order all the ingredients automatically. For instance, the computer knows exactly how much chocolate the store has on hand. It also knows how much chocolate will be used during any given period. Therefore, the computer can determine when to purchase more chocolate and how much to order.

The store manager sees the order on his screen. If it looks right, he lets the order go through to Park City. He can change it, if necessary, but the computer has done most of the work.

On the other hand, machines can't thoroughly train new employees. Only people can do that. Computers leave the store managers free to teach their bakers and salespeople.

FormMail and PhoneMail

FormMail is a computer program Mrs. Fields, Inc. uses for sending messages to and from the stores. It is a convenient way for store managers to communicate with the Park City staff. Employees send notes on every subject, including requests for pay raises. Debbi or an assistant answers every FormMail message within four days.

Store managers like the program because it gives them a chance to communicate directly with Debbi. One manager sent a request for ingredient lists. Some of her customers had food allergies. The lists would help them know which Mrs. Fields products they could safely eat.

Sometimes Debbi uses FormMail to find out what the competition is doing in different cities. She might ask a store manager in Chicago to check on a competing cookie store. The manager will visit the store, taste the products, and send Debbi a FormMail message. A typical report will include how the cookies taste, what they look like, and how much they cost.

For more urgent business, Debbi uses PhoneMail. This is a computer system that answers the phone, takes messages, plays them back, and transfers messages to the right people. PhoneMail puts Debbi's voice right into every store.

COMPUTER BENEFITS

Technology has allowed Mrs. Fields, Inc. to grow rapidly without adding large numbers of executives to run the company. In 1990, the Park City staff totaled 115 people. Without computer technology, Randy believes the executive staff would have been over 300.

At Park City headquarters, every key manager has a laptop computer. If managers enter Randy's office without their laptops, he sends them back for their machines. All ideas, suggestions, and requests must be stored in the computers.

Randy's laptop programs take the place of notepads, calculators, and phone books. They also help write reports and letters.

Computer link-ups with the cookie stores and bakeries give Park City managers instant feedback. Daily reports let them know if a store is in trouble. Debbi and her staff can give assistance before big problems have a chance to develop.

Records on every employee are also stored in the computer's memory. Computer programs help employees earn promotions. Quizzes and drills prepare them for jobs at higher levels.

Randy and Debbi even use the computer to decide where to expand. The computer advises which stores are making the most money and which are making the least. This information helps the company determine where to add new stores.

LEARNING THE SYSTEM

When Randy introduced his software program to the company, he urged Debbi to learn it. He knew the system would not succeed unless the head of the company used it. After her first lesson, Debbi was hooked. She stayed up until three o'clock in the morning entering her entire Day Planner.

Training Staff

Most inexperienced people are nervous when they begin using computers. The trick is to make it look easy. When people feel comfortable with the equipment, they'll use it efficiently.

Randy believes experts are the worst people to teach beginners. He thinks the best training comes from employees who are already using the system. They can encourage their co-workers and help them relax.

At Mrs. Fields, Inc., every employee receives a disk with four games. Beginners play computer games to become familiar with the machine. After a couple of hours playing games, they are ready for serious training. The company offers courses regularly. Debbi encourages everyone to learn one or two new skills every so often.

One rule Randy tries to follow is to keep technology as simple as possible. If it becomes too complicated, people will have trouble using it. The company keeps all its information stored on one data base. Cookie sales, salaries, bills, every type of information is on one program.

This means nobody wastes time entering the same information into more than one program. And no matter how much information someone needs, it's all available on the same program.

Keyboard Gurus

Randy started a **guru** department to help employees solve computer problems quickly. Anyone who is crazy about computers can be hired as a guru. Randy hires kids who work part time or summers. One of his best gurus is a high school dropout who is a whiz on the computer.

Today, Randy is chairman of the board and chief financial officer of Mrs. Fields, Inc. He also started a software company that develops computer systems for other companies.

Randy is well-known for computerizing Mrs. Fields, Inc. One economist says that Randy's system shows how tomorrow's businesses will be run.

Chapter 6

Recipe for Success

Americans spend about three billion dollars a year on cookies. Most of these cookies are supermarket products, with chocolate chip cookies the run-away favorites.

Approximately $250 million is spent in specialty stores each year for fresh-baked cookies. Mrs. Fields, David's Cookies, Famous Amos, and the Original Cookie Company are just a few specialty cookie companies.

Mrs. Field's Cookies leads them all in sales. It is the world's largest supplier of fresh-baked cookies. For her achievements, Debbi Fields has received dozens of honors and awards, including Woman of the Year, 1986; Outstanding Woman of America, 1986; and Distinguished Woman Award, 1988.

She was also named one of the "100 Greatest Entrepreneurs of the Last 25 Years" by author David Silver. He

Debbi's recipe for success is, "Do what you love to do!" (UPI/Bettmann.)

chose only six women for his book, *Entrepreneurial Megabucks*. Debbi and Liz Claiborne were two of those women.

Debbi and Randy Fields have been featured in leading magazines and newspapers. *People, Good Housekeeping, Fortune,* and *Forbes* magazines are just a few.

THE RIGHT INGREDIENTS

Debbi's cookie recipes are a well-kept secret, but she is eager to share her recipe for success.

Be yourself. Do what you love to do. Do what you do best and always try to do better.
Have faith in your goals even if they aren't what your family and friends expect of you.

Refuse to take no for an answer. Keep plugging away, one step at a time. If you believe strongly in what you're doing, the people around you begin to share your confidence.

Don't be afraid of failure. Learn from your mistakes.

BE A RISK TAKER! The best idea in the world isn't worth anything if you aren't willing to take a chance. Most successful entrepreneurs thrive under pressure and meeting challenges.

Think of success in terms of what you contribute. If you measure yourself in terms of money, you'll never be satisfied.

Putting It All Together

People kept telling Debbi to keep her business life separate from her personal life. But Debbi knew this wouldn't work for her. Mrs. Fields, Inc. is incredibly successful because Debbi's heart and soul are in the company.

Debbi's business goals and the way she runs the company are based on the kind of person she wants to be. "We're a people company," she says. "What we really do is take care of people." Debbi is truly concerned about her employees' personal lives.

Mrs. Fields cookies have to be perfect. But Debbi understands mistakes. She has overbaked or underbaked plenty of cookies herself. Debbi is convinced people will do their very best as long as they receive the right support. And she's always available to give it to them.

Debbi believes her role is to make people feel important and to create opportunities for them. She treats her employees the way she expects them to treat the customers – with warmth, kindness, and respect.

SHARING SUCCESS

Debbi and Randy Fields are grateful for their good fortune. They want to give something back to their community. Neither one takes a salary from the company; they have what they need. For them, the future involves more giving than taking.

Debbi and Randy established the Mrs. Fields Children's Health Foundation. Eighty percent of Mrs. Fields public stock is held in **trust** for the foundation. This means when Randy and Debbi die, the bulk of their fortune will be used to help poor, sick, and abused children.

For the past ten years, Debbi and Randy have also contributed millions of dollars to children's hospitals and services. Debbi is a member of the Board of Governors of LDS Hospital and the Primary Children's Foundation Medical Center in Salt Lake City, Utah.

But the cause dearest to Debbi's heart is the Cystic Fibrosis Foundation. Cystic fibrosis is a terrible children's disease with no known cure. The man who designed the Mrs. Fields corporate symbol had a daughter who died of the disease. Debbi and Randy were so touched by the tragedy that they vowed to help find a cure. Debbi serves as a director of the Cystic Fibrosis Research Foundation, to which she and Randy have donated over five million dollars.

Setting Up a Trust

Sometimes individuals or organizations set aside a portion of their wealth or property to be held in trust for another individual or group. The owner usually controls this trust as long as he or she lives. When the owner dies, the trust becomes the sole property of the individual or group for whom it was created.

Debbi doesn't want to be remembered for how many cookie stores she had. "Wouldn't it be great," she says, "if I could help find a cure for cystic fibrosis? I'd like to believe in my lifetime I really did something good.

"The main thing is if you absolutely know what you're doing is good . . . it's easy not to give up because you know you're going to make the world a little bit better."

Glossary

arcade   A covered passageway or street, often with shops on either side.

capital   Money, goods, or property used to produce an income.

competition   Economic rivalry between businesses that sell the same goods or services.

competitive   Involving rivalry or competition between people or businesses.

consumers   Those who use up goods that are produced.

data base   A large collection of specialized information organized in a computer to be retrieved quickly.

diversifying   Adding new activities or products.

entrepreneur   A person who organizes, controls, and takes all the risks of running a business.

financial consultant   A person who gives advice on money matters.

franchise   The right given to an individual or group to sell a company's goods or services in a particular area.

free market economy   An economic system in which supply and demand determine the price of goods or services.

guru   A respected teacher or leader.

image   A picture or impression that a person or organization gives of itself.

marketing   The advertising and selling of products or services.

profit   The money left over from selling goods or services after expenses are subtracted.

promote   To try to sell or increase the popularity of something.

quota   A fixed amount of sales required of a person or group.

retailing   The selling of goods or services to consumers for personal use.

specialty store   One that sells a particular type of product.

stock   A certificate of ownership in a company.

trust   Property or money held in safekeeping by another person or an institution, such as a bank.

Index